Portraits in Song

Great Spirituals

An Anthology or Program for Solo Voice and Piano
for Concert and Worship

Compiled and Edited by Andy Albritton

7 Favorite Spirituals with Reproducible Program Notes

Featuring Arrangements by

- **Tom Fettke**

- **Mark Hayes**

- **Larry Shackley**

- **Jean Anne Shafferman**

- **Robert Sterling**

Book:
ISBN-10: 0-7390-4835-X
ISBN-13: 978-0-7390-4835-1
Book and Accompaniment CD:
ISBN-10: 0-7390-4836-8
ISBN-13: 978-0-7390-4836-8
Accompaniment CD:
ISBN-10: 0-7390-4837-6
ISBN-13: 978-0-7390-4837-5

Alfred Publishing Co., Inc.
16320 Roscoe Blvd., Suite 100
P.O. Box 10003
Van Nuys, CA 91410-0003

Alfred

alfred.com

Table of Contents

Foreword

The *Spiritual* has witnessed an extraordinary historical journey. It is the testament of a strong, faith-filled people who, amidst the wretched inhumanity of slavery, emerged with songs of endurance, survival, hope, and even joy. It is also commonly considered the first *truly* American folk music.

As with any song, there are two basic elements that can be examined, lyric and melody. Typically, one would expect that both lyric and melody, in any given case, would be similar in mood. For example, if the lyrics spoke of hope or joy, the melody would reinforce the sentiment. Though there are many examples of spirituals that do just that, exceptions emerge in great number, especially with the slower, "anthem" spiritual.

In *Slave Songs of the United States*, the first major academic work on the subject of spirituals, we read the following written in 1867, just a couple of years after the close of the American Civil War (1861–1865) and the ratification of the Thirteenth Amendment (1865) which abolished slavery in the U.S.

> *The wild, sad strains tell, as the sufferers themselves could, of crushed hopes, keen sorrow, and a dull daily misery, which covered them as hopelessly as the fog from the rice swamps. On the other hand, the words breathe a trusting faith in the rest of the future—in 'Canaan's (f)air and happy land,' to which their eyes seem constantly turned.* (**Slaves Songs of the United States**, *1867, Allen, Ware & Garrison, pg. xix)*

Though there are composers still writing in the "spiritual style" today, one should not confuse these new compositions with the original spirituals (*a.k.a. Traditional or Negro Spirituals*) composed prior to the abolition of slavery (1865) and compositions or arrangements based on the originals. The titles contained in this book belong to the latter distinction, being arrangements of original spirituals. I hope that as you experience these spirituals in worship or recital, you will give ear and heart to the original singers of these songs, be inspired by their hope, and enlivened by their joy amidst tremendous hardship. And more so, may you see the enduring relevance of this distinctly human song.

Andy Albritton, Editor

Acknowledgements

Mr. Albritton wishes to thank the following for their input and invaluable assistance: Jean Anne Shafferman, Tom Goeman, Kent Heckman at Red Rock Recording (Saylorsburg, PA), Bruce Goldes, Matt Koprowski, and Reynold Furrell.

To my friends in the music ministry at Willow Creek Community Church,
South Barrington, Illinois

Give Me Jesus

Traditional Spiritual
Arranged by Larry Shackley (ASCAP)

Also available for S.A.T.B. voices, No. 20992,
and S.A.B. voices, No. 20993.

world. You can have all this world,_____ but give me Je - sus, give me Je - sus, give me Je - sus!_____

Were You There?

Traditional Spiritual
Arranged by Larry Shackley (ASCAP)

Also available for S.A.T.B. voices, No. 23617,
and 2-Part mixed voices, No. 26318.

26382

Here's One

Traditional Spiritual
Arranged by Tom Fettke

Also available for S.A.T.B. voices, No. 26466,
and S.A.B. voices, No. 26467.

In memory of Fred Bock (1939–1998)

Carry Me Home

Incorporating *Deep River* and
Swing Low, Sweet Chariot

Arranged by
Jean Anne Shafferman

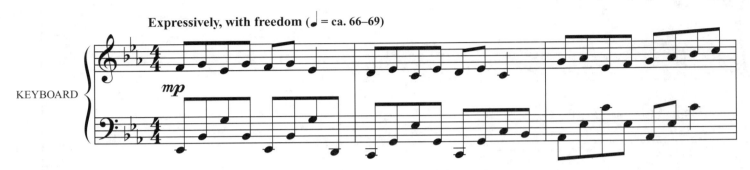

Also available for S.A.T.B. voices, No. 18926, S.A.B. voices, No. 18927,
and 2-Part any combination of voices, No. 18928.

want to cross o - ver in - to camp - ground.

O, don't you want to go to that

gos - pel feast, that

prom - ised land where all is

26382

Every Time I Feel the Spirit

Traditional Spiritual
Arranged by Mark Hayes

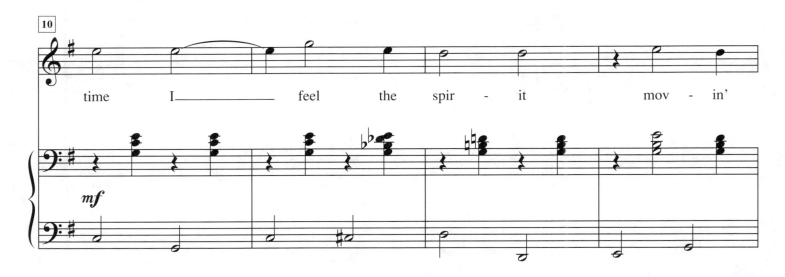

in my heart,_____ I will pray._____ Ev - 'ry

time I feel the spir - it mov - in'

in my heart, I will pray. Up on the

moun - tain my Lord spoke. Out of His

in my heart,_____ I will pray._____ Ev - 'ry

time I feel the spir - it mov - in'

in my heart, I will pray. There ain't but

one train on this track. It runs to

*Cue note may be sung as an option.

Go, Tell It on the Mountain

Traditional Spiritual
Arranged by Robert Sterling

ev - 'ry - where.___ Go, tell it on the moun - tain___ that

Je - sus Christ_is born.___ Down in a low - ly

(even eighths)

man - ger the hum - ble Christ was born,___ and

God sent us sal - va - tion___ that bless - ed

poco a poco cresc.

58

Christ - mas morn!

61 Jazz swing *mf*

Go, tell it on the

62

moun - tain,— o - ver the hills and ev - 'ry - where.— Go, tell it on the

66

moun - tain— that Je - sus Christ is born!

69 *f*

Go, tell it on the moun - tain,— o - ver the hills and

Joshua Fit the Battle of Jericho

Traditional Spiritual
Arranged by Mark Hayes

Program Notes

Spirituals arose as an organic song form from an oral tradition, so knowing specifics about composers, lyricists, and any particular back-story is challenging. Even if a slave were inclined to write down a song that he or she penned, it would have been against the law, as literacy — and indeed, any sort of formal education — was forbidden and subject to severe punishment. So, we will never know with certainty the identity of those responsible for specific songs. However, educated guesses can be made as to the geographical region of origin and the type of spiritual — relating to how a song was used.

Give Me Jesus

Some spirituals seemed to be based on hymns that were heard or, more frequently, overheard at the 'white' churches. Though unsubstantiated, with its regular meter and melodic scheme, *Give Me Jesus* seems an obvious candidate. Because of this *familiar* sound, it was also one of the first spirituals to be included in a hymnal and was a favorite among church goers. The original verses were as follows:

Verse 1 Oh, when I come to die…

Verse 2 I heard my mother say…

Verse 3 Dark midnight was my cry…

Verse 4 In the morning when I rise…

Verse 5 I heard the mourner say…

Were You There?

Upon arrival in what is now the United States, a slave was not allowed to practice African religions or customs. In a manipulative effort, a plantation owner would Christianize his subjects as quickly as possible, reciting the Old Testament references of *accepted* slavery and the *proper* respect a slave was expected to have for his master. However, what the owner did not foresee was how readily the persecuted slave identified with Christ and His suffering. For in the story of Jesus, one hears of a man who was misunderstood, unjustly imprisoned, tortured, and executed. Slaves believed that this

Jesus was someone who understood suffering, and more so, they could understand His. Theologically speaking, with an intimate understanding of suffering, as a slave pondered the question, "Were you there when they crucified my Lord?" the obvious answer was, "Yes, I was (and continue to be) *there*."

Here's One

The musical scale given to us by western tradition is inadequate to accurately render a spiritual. As in the modern-day descendant, jazz (or blues), the spiritual frequently employs the *blue* note. Most commonly the *blue* note refers to the flatted third or seventh step of the western seven note scale. However, the real (or historic) *blue* note falls between the gaps of the accepted western scale. It is only "in the gaps" that the mournful, soulful, and truly *blue* note sounds. It must be remembered that spirituals were sung accompanied only by hand claps, moans, stomps, or dancing. Thus, there were no fixed-scale instruments to imprison the tone. In *Here's One* we hear an example of the soulful blue note — in this case, the flatted third scale step.

Carry Me Home

(Incorporating *Deep River* and
    Swing Low, Sweet Chariot)
Both *Deep River* and *Swing Low, Sweet Chariot* were significant to those enslaved, because while singing of religious themes, they also carried hidden messages.

The "Jordan (River)" mentioned in *Deep River* clandestinely refers to the Ohio, Mississippi, or any other river which could be a means of escape and whose crossing meant freedom. Slave owners assumed that slaves were only singing of Biblical stories or baptism. But to a slave contemplating a dangerous escape, knowledge of rivers was vital. Rivers provided direction and a means of navigation — even on a cloudy night. For a slave in the Deep South, following a river upstream usually meant north, which would eventually lead to freedom. Also, the most effective way of losing a pack of tracking bloodhounds was to "wade in the water". So while the *river* has biblical and theological implications, it also is surreptitiously instructional.

Swing Low, Sweet Chariot was a favorite of the Underground Railroad (a network of slave sympathizers and abolitionists who helped escaping slaves by smuggling them out of the South). In fact, the "Chariot" directly refers to the "Railroad". This spiritual was frequently sung to alert slaves that an escape had been planned and/or the time to leave was eminent. Again, the slave owners simply thought the slaves were singing about a Biblical story.

Every Time I Feel the Spirit

Once a week in the evening, slaves would usually meet in the designated *praise-house* to have a *sing* or *praise-night*. When the formal service was over, the benches would be pushed up against the wall and a "sperichil" would be *struck up*. The attendees would organize themselves into a semblance of a circle and begin to shuffle around the center of the room. As the evening progressed regular "sperichils" would be replaced with "runnin' sperichils" (or *shouts*). *Every Time I Feel the Spirit* could easily be sung as one of these "runnin' sperichils." A designated singer (shouter) would chant the verses and the entire assembly would "join in" on the chorus. These energetic *praise-house* meetings would typically continue for half the night.

Go, Tell It on the Mountain

This spiritual, certainly the most popular among the Christmas spirituals, is attributed to the educator and African-American folk music preservationist, John Wesley Work, Jr. (1872–1925). Though he did not compose the spiritual, he did arrange it into the form that we hear today. Work graduated and taught at the first university in the U.S. dedicated to African-American education, Fisk University in Nashville, Tennessee. Interestingly, the institution, founded in January 1866, began its instruction in buildings which were abandoned Union Army barracks vacated just six months before, at the end of the American Civil War (1861–1865).

Fisk University and the Fisk University Jubilee Singers are responsible for an immeasurable contribution to the preservation of the spiritual. Four short years after Fisk University opened its doors it seemed that lack of finances would close the institution. In an effort to save the school, the Jubilee Singers were formed to raise much needed funds. After an underwhelming first few concerts, the Singers revised their repertoire to include "slave songs" or spirituals. The response was so enthusiastic that after seven years and two European tours they had raised over $150,000 dollars for their school, thus saving their school and exposing the world to this remarkable song genre.

Joshua Fit the Battle of Jericho

Joshua, as well as many other Old Testament "fighting" characters, was a favorite of spiritual writers, representing triumph over seemingly overwhelming adversity. These stories and spirituals were used by slaves to encourage one another to keep their eyes focused on the inevitable reward of the "promised land." In the slave's case the first foretaste of the "promised land" was freedom and an end to their daily suffering. This song is classified as a *runnin' sperichil* or *shout*, (verses a regular *sit-down sperichil* or *anthem*) as it could be used in a *praise-house* meeting, accompanied by dancing and clapping.

About the Editor

Andy Albritton is Church Choral Editor for Alfred Publishing Company and holds a Bachelor of Music in Music Composition from Mississippi College and a Master of Music in Choral Music from the University of Southern California. He is a well-respected composer/arranger and has published works for choir, blended/contemporary worship, and vocal soloists. Mr. Albritton resides in Southern California and serves as Worship Director at Holy Trinity Church in Ladera Ranch.

About the Arrangers

Tom Fettke is a well-known composer, arranger and producer of music and recordings for church and school. Widely published, his music has been performed by thousands of choirs throughout the world. In considerable demand as a guest conductor, clinician and worship leader, he also has served as Senior Editor for several distinguished hymnals. A church choir director and minister of music in churches large and small for over 30 years, Tom lives in Brentwood, Tennessee.

Mark Hayes is an award-winning concert pianist, composer and arranger of choral, piano and orchestral music. With over 550 published works to his credit, Mark has also recorded numerous solo piano albums and has received the Gospel Music Association's prestigious Dove Award, which is equivalent to a Grammy in gospel music. A graduate of Baylor University, he has served as an adjunct professor of composition at Midwestern Baptist Theological Seminary in Kansas City, Missouri.

Larry Shackley directs the music program at Columbia (SC) International University and holds a D.M.A. in composition from the University of South Carolina. Previously, he was staff composer for Moody Broadcasting in Chicago, and keyboardist/arranger at Willow Creek Community Church (South Barrington, IL). His choral and keyboard arrangements, broadcast themes and film scores have been heard around the world.

Jean Anne Shafferman is Director of Church Choral Publications for Alfred Publishing Company. A graduate of the University of Kentucky with a B.M.E. in vocal music education and an M.A. in music theory, she is active as a church musician, clinician and composer, and has served as the Eastern Division Music in Worship Chairperson for the American Choral Directors' Association.

Robert Sterling is a Dove Award winning composer, arranger and record producer whose songs have been recorded by a variety of Christian artists. A widely published church choral composer and orchestrator, he led the songwriting faculty for the Academy of Gospel Music Arts for five years. A graduate of Baylor University, he has also served as an adjunct professor of Music Publishing at Belmont University in Nashville.